CAST

Ronkẹ Adékoluẹjo | Her

Ronkẹ Adékoluẹjo's theatre credits include: *Three Sisters* (National Theatre, for which she won the 3rd prize Ian Charleson Award), *Cyprus Avenue* (Royal Court, Abbey, Dublin and Public, New York), *Hole and Bad Roads* (Royal Court), *The Mountaintop* (Young Vic), *Twelfth Night* (Filter and on USA and India tour), *The Oresteia* (HOME Manchester), *Pride and Prejudice* (Sheffield Crucible), *The House That Will Not Stand and The Colby Sisters of Pittsburgh Pennsylvania* (Kiln), *Anon* (Theatre Royal Plymouth), *Random* (Crooked Path).

She plays the series regular of Jack Starbright in *Alex Rider* (Amazon Prime), she also appeared in *Cuckoo, Doctor Who, NW, Cold Feet, Sick Note, Josh, Chewing Gum, Suspects* and *The Forgiving Earth*.

Her film credits include *Ear for Eye, Christopher Robin, Been So Long, Ready Player One, One Crazy Thing, Lascivious Grace, The Forgotten C, Broken* and *The Big Other*.

CREATIVE TEAM

Benedict Lombe | Writer

Benedict Lombe is a Kinshasa-born, Congolese British writer based in London.

She has been on attachment at the Bush Theatre as part of the Emerging Writers Group, completed a residency at Theatre503 as part of the 503Five and also taken part in the BBC Writersroom programme. She has produced digital work for the Bush as part of *The Protest* series, Papatango Theatre Company as part of *Isolated But Open*, and a site-specific piece as part of Damsel Productions' *Outdoors* season. *Lava*, produced at the Bush Theatre, is her debut play.

She is currently working on developing original TV projects, with a focus on boldly reclaiming diasporic stories that were never allowed to be told, with the full shades of nuance they always deserved.

Anthony Simpson-Pike | Director

Anthony Simpson-Pike is a director, dramaturg and writer whose work has been staged in theatres including the Gate Theatre, Young Vic and Royal Court. He is currently Associate Director at The Yard Theatre, was previously the Resident Director at Theatre Peckham and was Associate Director at the Gate. Anthony is also a facilitator, working with young people and communities, having worked at the Gate, Royal Court, Young Vic, Sjhakespeare's Globe and National Theatre in this capacity.

In addition to theatre, Anthony has worked with Tamasha Theatre company to make audio dramas including collaborations with the National Archives on projects such as *Loyalty and Dissent* and *Once British, Always British* and enjoys working across different media including film, having worked on *Ear for Eye* by debbie tucker green for BBC Films and BFI. He is passionate about international work, having received a British Council bursary to visit the Informal European Theatre Meeting in Brussels, as well as being selected by the British Council to attend DirectorsLab North in Toronto. In 2019, he was invited to be a visiting guest artist for the Banff Playwrights Lab. He is also working on the international project for the Royal Court in Jamaica and Barbados.

Recent directorial work includes: *The Ridiculous Darkness* by Wolfram Lotz at the Gate, which received five-star reviews, 'stunning and subversive' (*The Stage*), 'you'd be sorely pressed to find anything more riveting or stupendous' (WhatsOnStage.com).

Jasmine Swan | Designer

Jasmine Swan trained at Liverpool Insititute for Performing Arts, receiving the Ede & Ravenscroft Prize for Creative & Technical Excellence (2016). She was a Linbury Prize finalist in 2017, and has been nominated for The Stage Debut Awards 2018 and OffWestEnd Awards. She was the Laboratory Associate Designer for Nuffield Southampton Theatres in 2017/18.

Credits include: *Animal Farm* (Royal & Derngate, National Youth Theatre), *Lady Chatterley's Lover* (Shaftesbury Theatre), *Earthquakes in London*, *Little Shop of Horrors* (LAMDA), *Shook* (Southwark Playhouse), *Armadillo* (The Yard), *Women In Power* (Nuffield Southampton Theatres and Oxford Playhouse), *Eden* (Hampstead Theatre), *The Tide Jetty* (Eastern Angles Touring Theatre), *Sex Sex Men Men* (Pecs Drag Kings), *Sonny* (Arts Educational Schools), *Son Of Rambow* (The Other Palace), *Chutney* (The Bunker), *i* (Theatre503).

Jai Morjaria | Lighting Designer

Jai Morjaria trained at RADA and won the 2016 Association of Lighting Designer's ETC Award.

Recent designs include: *Cruise* (Duchess Theatre), *Pawn/Limbo* (Bush Theatre), *The Hoes* (Hampstead Theatre), *My Son's A Queer (But What Can You Do?)* (Turbine Theatre), *Hushabye Mountain* (Hope Mill), *Out of the Dark* (Rose Theatre Kingston), *Shuck'n'Jive*, *Whitewash* (Soho Theatre), *Anansi the Spider*, *Aesop's Fables* (Unicorn Theatre), *World's End* (King's Head Theatre), *I'll Take You to Mrs Cole!* (Complicité), *The Actor's Nightmare* (Park Theatre), *Mapping Brent* (Kiln Theatre), *Mary's Babies* (Jermyn Street Theatre), *Glory* (Duke's Theatre/Red Ladder), *Cuzco* (Theatre503), *Losing Venice* (Orange Tree Theatre), *King Lear*, *Lorna Doone* (Exmoor National Park), *Cinderella* (Duke's Lancaster), *A Lie of the Mind* (Southwark Playhouse), *46 Beacon* (Trafalgar Studios), *Out There on Fried Meat Ridge Road* (White Bear Theatre, Trafalgar Studio 2), *Acorn* (Courtyard Theatre; Off-West End Award nomination for Best Lighting).

Josh Anio Grigg | Sound Designer

Josh Anio Grigg mainly works in the medium of sound, but also includes other new media practices as well as arts facilitation ideas into his projects.

In 2008 he completed a Drama, Theatre and Performance degree at Roehampton University of Surrey.

Theatre credits include: *Faith, Hope and Charity* (National Theatre, European tour), *The End of Eddy* (Unicorn), *The Unknown Island* (Gate), *Basic Tension* (ICA London), *Oliver Twist* (Regent's Park Open Air), *Love* (National Theatre, Birmingham Rep), *Beyond Caring* (National Theatre, Yard Theatre, UK tour, Chicago), *Dirty Crusty*, *The Crucible*, *A New and Better You*, *This Beautiful Future*, *Removal Men*, *Made Visible*, *Lines*, *ThevMikvah Project* (The Yard), *Parallel Macbeth* (Young Vic), *F*ck the Polar Bears* (Bush Theatre).

Gino Ricardo Green | Projection Designer

Gino Ricardo Green is a Director and Video/Projection designer, who co-founded Black Apron Entertainment. Credits Include: *Children's Children* (English Touring Theatre), *Beyond the Canon* (RADA), *Be More Chill* (The Other Palace), *Sweat* (West End and Donmar Warehouse), *Small Island* (National Theatre).

DK Fashola | Movement Director

DK Fashola is a multidisciplinary artist who specialises in multi-form storytelling; fusing movement, witty dialogue and poetic multilayered text in unexpected ways.

Work includes, as Director and Writer: *All The Things* (Arts Ed), *Fragments of a Complicated Mind* (Theatre503), *Scalped* (Without Walls national tour).

As Movement Director: *Othello* (NYTRep 21), *Birds & Bees* (Theatre Centre), *846Live* (TRSE), *Little Baby Jesus* (Orange Tree Theatre; Movement Consultant), and *Essence Exhibition* (Mr Eazi Culture Fest).

As Actress: *Nadia's Gift* (film, Jack Studio Theatre), *Mami Wata* (work-in-progress, Bush), *Ilé La Wà* (Stratford Circus), *Muscovado* (Burnt Out Theatre tour).

As Choreographer (Music Video): *Dis Love* (Wizkid), *Rushing* (Alicai Harley), *Olorun mi* (Tiwa Savage), *Don't Bother Me* (Shakka), *Pour Me Water* (Mr Eazi, official dance video)

She is Artistic Director of Initiative.dkf, creators of Melanin Box Festival, Albany Theatre's 2021 Artists of Change, and Tamasha Associate Artists ('19–'20)

Esi Acquaah-Harrison | Dialect Coach

Esi Acquaah-Harrison trained in Voice Studies at Royal Central School of Speech and Drama.

Credits and experience include: *Sex Education* (Season Three), *Punk Rock* (Stratford Circus), *Pigeon English* (Tobacco Factory), *The High Table* (Bush).

As a singer, Esi has a depth of experience including: *Cirque du Soleil – Totem* (world tour), and Rafiki in *The Lion King* (Disneyland Resort, Paris).

Deirdre O'Halloran | Dramaturg

Deirdre O'Halloran is the Literary Manager at the Bush Theatre, working to identify and build relationships with new writers, commission new work and guide plays to the stage. At the Bush she's dramaturged plays including Olivier Award-winner *Baby Reindeer* by Richard Gadd, *The High Table* by Temi Wilkey and *An Adventure* by Vinay Patel. Deirdre was previously Literary Associate at Soho Theatre, where she worked as a dramaturg on plays including *Girls* by Theresa Ikoko and *Fury* by Phoebe Eclair-Powell. She led on Soho Theatre's Writers' Lab programme and the biennial Verity Bargate Award. As a freelancer, Deirdre has also been a reader for Out of Joint, Sonia Friedman Productions and Papatango.

Chandra Ruegg | Casting

Chandra Ruegg started working in the industry as a child actress. After more than twenty years, she decided to move into the world of casting. Her first stint was assisting Amy Ball on *Dance Nation* at the Almeida Theatre. From there she assisted Charlotte Sutton at Chichester Festival Theatre for two seasons. For the screen, she has worked in the Casting offices of Nanw Rowlands assisting on *Outside the Wire* (Netflix), *Voyagers* (Lionsgate) and *Censor* (BFI), Andy Pryor, Lauren Evans and Olivia Scott Webb. As of January 2021 she became an associate for Sophie Holland Casting working on the Amazon series *The Peripheral* and Netflix/MGM series *Wednesday*. Chandra has cast various short films over the years. *Lava* is her first credit as a Casting Director for theatre.

Bush
Theatre
We make theatre
for London. Now.

The Bush is a world-famous home for new plays
and an internationally renowned champion of
playwrights. We discover, nurture and produce
the best new writers from the widest range of
backgrounds from our home in a distinctive corner
of west London.

The Bush has won over 100 awards and developed
an enviable reputation for touring its acclaimed
productions nationally and internationally.

We are excited by exceptional new voices,
stories and perspectives – particularly those with
contemporary bite which reflect the vibrancy of
British culture now.

Located in the newly renovated old library on
Uxbridge Road in the heart of Shepherd's Bush,
the theatre houses two performance spaces, a
rehearsal room and the lively Library Bar.

  bushtheatre.co.uk

Bush Theatre

Artistic Director	Lynette Linton
Executive Director	Lauren Clancy
Literary Assistant	Gift Ajimokun
Associate Director	Daniel Bailey
Senior Technician	Francis Botu
Senior Producer	Jessica Campbell
Digital Marketing Officer	Shannon Clarke
Development Officer	Florence Collenette
Assistant Venue Manager	Jack Cook
Head of Development	Ruth Davey
Marketing Consultant	Ali Forbes
Finance Assistant	Lauren Francis
Young Company Coordinator	Katie Greenall
Head of Finance	Neil Harris
Assistant Venue Manager	Isabele Hernandez
Digital Producer	Cheryl Jordan Osei
Deputy Venue Manager	Tim McNiven
Literary Manager	Deirdre O'Halloran
Associate Producer	Oscar Owen
Theatre Administrator and Event Producer	Jessica Pentney
Development Intern	Sabrina Pui Yee Chin
Press Manager	Martin Shippen
Community Producer	Holly Smith
Technical Manager	Ian Taylor
Marketing and Ticketing Officer	Ed Theakston
Community Intern	Erin Thorpe
Development Assistant	Eleanor Tindall
General Manager	Angela Wachner
Venue Manager	Barbara Zemper

Duty Managers
David Bolwell, Ilaria Ciardelli, Ryan Cottee, Marissa McKinnon and Eljai Morais

Bar Supervisors
Nieta Irons, Chantal-Carine Neckles, Melissa Stephen and Rafael Uzcategui

Box Office, Bar & Front of House Team
Roxane Cabassut, Lydia Feerick, Joshua Glenister, Kelsey Gordon, Matias Hailu, Olivia Hanrahan-Barnes, Judd Launder, Munaye Lichtenstein, Emily Orme, Max Partridge, Charlie Phillips, Humaira Wadiwala, Robin Wilks, Charlie Wood

Board of Trustees:
Simon Johnson (Chair), Simon Dowson-Collins, Uzma Hasan, Nia Janis, Nike Jonah, Lynette Linton, Kathryn Marten, Raj Parkash, Stephen Pidcock and Catherine Score

Bush Theatre, 7 Uxbridge Road, London W12 8LJ
Box Office: 020 8743 5050 | Administration: 020 8743 3584
Email: info@bushtheatre.co.uk
bushtheatre.co.uk

Alternative Theatre Company Ltd
The Bush Theatre is a Registered Charity and a company limited by guarantee.
Registered in England no. 1221968 Charity no. 270080

THANK YOU

The Bush Theatre would like to thank all its supporters whose valuable contributions have helped us to create a platform for our future and to promote the highest quality new writing, develop the next generation of creative talent, lead innovative community engagement work and champion diversity.

MAJOR DONORS
Gianni & Michael Alen-Buckley
Charles Holloway
Georgia Oetker
Tim & Cathy Score
Jack Thorne

LONE STARS
Gianni Alen-Buckley
Michael Alen-Buckley
Jacqui Bull
Rafael & Anne-Helene Biosse Duplan
Charles Holloway
Priscilla John
Rosemary Morgan
Georgia Oetker
Susie Simkins

HANDFUL OF STARS
Charlie Bigham
Judy Bollinger
Clyde Cooper
Sue Fletcher
Joanna Kennedy
Simon & Katherine Johnson
Garry Lawrence
V&F Lukey
Anthony Marraccino
Aditya Mittal
Robert Ledger & Sally Moulsdale
Clare Rich
Lesley Hill & Russ Shaw
Kit and Anthony Van Tulleken

RISING STARS
Holly & Bruno Albutt
David Brooks
Catharine Browne
Matthew Byam Shaw
Philip Cameron & Richard Smith
Esperanza Cerdan
Grace Chan
Lauren Clancy
Tim & Andrea Clark
Sarah Clarke
Claude & Suzanne Cochin de Billy
Susie Cuff
Matthew Cushen
Philippa Dolphin
Sarah Edwards
Jack Gordon & Kate Lacy
Hugh & Sarah Grootenhuis
Thea Guest
Fiona l'Anson
Davina & Malcolm Judelson
Lynette Linton
Miggy Littlejohns
Judith Mellor
Caro Millington
Danny Morrison
Dan & Laurie Mucha
Rajiv Parkash
Mark & Anne Paterson
Brian Smith
Joe Tinston & Amelia Knott
Peter Tausig
Jan Topham
Guy Vincent & Sarah Mitchell

CORPORATE SPONSORS
Biznography
Dorsett Shepherds Bush
Jamie Lloyd Company
Studio Doug
U+I
Wychwood Media

TRUSTS AND FOUNDATIONS
29th May 1961 Charitable Trust
Christina Smith Foundation
Cockayne Foundation - Grants for the Arts
The Daisy Trust
Esmee Fairbairn
Foyle Foundation
Garfield Weston Foundation
Hammersmith United Charities
The Harold Hyam Wingate Foundation
John Lyon's Charity
Leche Trust
The Martin Bowley Charitable Trust
One anonymous donor
Orange Tree Trust
Royal Victoria Hall Foundation
The Teale Charitable Trust
Tudor Trust
Victoria Wood Foundation

Supported by
ARTS COUNCIL ENGLAND

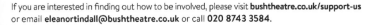

If you are interested in finding out how to be involved, please visit **bushtheatre.co.uk/support-us** or email **eleanortindall@bushtheatre.co.uk** or call **020 8743 3584**.

LAVA

Benedict Lombe

Thanks

I am grateful to so many people who nurtured my mind and my soul, allowing this play to come into existence.

My parents; my Mama and Papa, whose refusal to settle taught me bravery before I even had the words for it. My brothers, my co-conspirators, who turned the cross-continental journeys we undertook into unforgettable adventures. My nephews, whose joy, wit and spark push me to fight for a world that might one day be deserving of them. And Paddy Gervers, whose remarkable kindness, patience and care held me throughout this process.

Dan Bailey, thank you for starting this journey with me; for always allowing me to tell this story with integrity and never wavering in your trust in what this could become. Deirdre O'Halloran, thank you for your wisdom. Lynette Linton and the entire Bush Theatre Team, thank you for welcoming me and this play into your house.

And last, but never least, Anthony Simpson-Pike and Ronkẹ Adékoluẹjo. You are magic.

– Bx.

For my people:

the ones who paved the way
the ones who walk alongside me now
and the ones who will come after us.

Notes on the Play

Speech in *italics* should be pre-recorded audio by other voices.

Scenes are numbered in the text but intended to flow into each other.

A full stop between lines indicates a new thought or swift passage of time.

Speech in brackets can be a shift in tone or under the breath (like a side-note).

Words in ***italics and bold*** are song lyrics.

Staging

This play can be staged however you see fit.

In our production, the stage became a lava lake.

Rusted pillars jutted out of the ground and volcanic rock was peppered all around.

A giant cardboard box, half-melting into the lava, towered over everything like a volcano.

This text went to press before the end of rehearsals and so may differ slightly from the play as performed.

Characters

A Black woman plays all characters.

HER, *late twenties, Black woman (London accent of choice)*

MAMA, *mid-fifties, Black woman (Congolese accent)*

PARTNER, *late twenties, white man (East London Cockney accent)*

AFRIKANER TEACHER, *late thirties, white woman (Afrikaner accent)*

SOUTH AFRICAN TEACHER, *late thirties, Black woman (Zulu or Sotho accent)*

DOCTOR, *late forties, white woman (RP accent)*

Recorded Voice-overs

PASSPORT OFFICE, *mid-thirties, white man (RP accent)*

THEM, *late twenties, white man and/or woman (various British accents)*

PUPIL 1, *thirteen, white girl (Northern accent)*

PUPIL 2, *thirteen, white boy (Northern accent)*

REPORTER, *late thirties, white woman (RP accent)*

JOURNO 1, *mid-thirties, white man (West London accent)*

JOURNO 2, *late thirties, white woman (East London accent)*

PRODUCER, *mid-fifties, white woman (West London accent)*

L.A. PRODUCER, *late forties, white man (American accent)*

PREFACE
The Thread

ONE

*An upbeat pop cover of Aretha Franklin's 'Think' by H.E.R
plays in the background. Maybe people are still taking their
seats. The play has not yet begun.*

*There is a seamless transition as this song goes from being
background house music to being part of the play.*
*Perhaps the actor has been sitting in the audience and now goes
onstage. The lights should not go down. It should feel like she is
casually stepping into her own space, her own memory, her own
personal mixtape.*

*She starts vibing to the music. Plays it cool at first. Freestyling.
She's good, actually. Really good.*

'Think about what you're tryna do to me.'

*Then she drops the pretence and starts doing the most.
Her freestyle morphs into recognisable dance routines
popularised by Black people.*
*Think viral TikTok dances before TikTok. Maybe we see the Jerk.
The Dougie. The Stanky Leg. Then she hits the Woah. The Nae
Nae. The Dab. Sis throws it back. Bodies the Ndombolo.
We ain't ready.*

'Gimme some freedoooooom!'

*She's simultaneously having fun with it and taking it very
seriously. Think celebs with no chill on* Lip Sync Battle.

*Every now and then, she throws us a look – a hint that she might
be messing with us but isn't ready to let us in on the joke just yet.*

She stops. She's out of breath.
She's acting bait about waiting for applause.
*Maybe she gets a response and she tries to goad a bigger
response.*
*Maybe she gets a bigger response and she's still feeling hella
petty:*

HER.   Nah, you lot. Too slow, man.

            Maybe the lights go down.
            Maybe you do whatever the hell you want.
            And the play begins.

TWO

HER.   Hello. (*Waits for response.*)
Alright? (*Waits again.*)
This is nice, innit? Yeah.
Good little set-up to tell you the story of my
name.
The story of my true name.

Beat.

It begins with me applying to renew my
British passport for the first time.
A process that should've been straightforward,
became anything but.
Became messy and tangled.
Snagging and knotting up.
Demanding that I follow the thread
to find the knot
that would unravel the mess. So I did.
I followed the thread and it led me back to
these places.
Places I called 'elsewheres'.
Places I'd grown up and come of age in.
Places that now weaved in and around each
other, threading all the way through to the
present.
Yesterday and today wrapping around each
other tightly
tying a knot with the smallest opening for
tomorrow
and meeting us right here.
Right now.

Beat.

Shall we then?

THREAD ONE
Congo: What's in a name?

ONE

PASSPORT
OFFICE.   *'Dear Miss Her Last Name*

Re: Passport Application for
Miss Her First Name, Her Middle Name, Her
Last Name.

For us to re-issue a British passport in the
name of
"Her First Name, Her Middle Name, Her Last
Name",
you need to change the name shown on your
South African passport and then send it to us
at the address shown at the end of this letter.

Please stick the attached label and
appropriate postage to the outside of your
reply envelope.

We look forward to hearing from you soon.

Yours sincerely,
Her Majesty's Passport Office.'

HER.   Hit the first snag. I'm a dual citizen.
                 British. And South African.
                 Neither by heritage nor birth.
                 A citizen of two nations
                 in which I hold no roots.

So I get this letter. And this letter makes me...
pause (*She pauses*.)
And I wanna say it's 'graceful'... yeah, think
old Hollywood glamour.
Think: 'beautiful woman staring out of
window, chin angled upward
with that quizzical slash mildly constipated
look men write poems about'.
And if, say, I 'on't know, the reality was more
like:
'woman lying upside down in holey old
underwear as partner comes up with Friday
night curry,' who's to know, *really*?

So I'm reading this letter and yo, lemme tell
you: I'm *triggered*.
I grew up with passports being very serious
business.
Like *surrr-ious* serious.
And whenever we moved somewhere new –
which formed the basis of my entire childhood
– my parents would make such a *thing* about
collecting our passports when it was 'time'.
And it was always urgent and big and scary
and for real felt like a kind of punishment,
right, like an obstacle course you had to
endure
and if you played your cards right
and if you didn't give up
and if you had enough money
and if you had enough access
and if you were the 'right' type of person
and if you were blah blah blah
and passed 'Go' after your round of
Monopoly, you could collect two hundred and
your shiny new passport.

As a kid, all of it translated into:
'This is looooooooooooong, man.'

And also:
'Why are there no crisps?'

But I'd never forget that feeling of urgency
around these tiny documents. And when I
complained about standing in long queues and
having my photos taken and my fingerprints
pressed onto form after form and asking
(*Crying*.) 'why Mama, whyyyyyy though?'
I'll never forget what she said:

MAMA.   'This document is your proof. This document
               is your protection.'

               Beat.

HER.   That changed things. Later. Way way later (in
               that moment, I'm still a kid, and nowhere in
               her response did she reveal where the crisps
               were, so frankly, give a shit?).

               It would be years later when I would finally
               understand how my parents saw passports.
               As the document that recognised your
               permission to *exist*. Permission to be counted.
               They remembered a not-so-distant past when
               Africans were forced to carry identity passes
               at all times, to prove their legitimacy in their
               own countries, or risk being arrested.

               Beat.

               So. *Surrr-ious* serious. And I'm reading this
               letter and that's all I'm thinking – urgent and
               scary and big and important and *jail*, okay,
               I'm thinking *jail*, and my brain goes into
               overdrive because now this feels like the
               ultimate rejection of my permission to exist.
               So I turn to my partner, this poor unsuspecting

man who has dealt with years of my holey
underwear with such grace, I turn to him,
right, and I just let loose:

'I knew it, I knew it, fucking *knew* it! And
I said. Didn't I? That they'd come up with
something? I said! And they did, and I fucking
knew it!'

And my partner takes the letter and reads it
and dares (dares!) to say something sensible
and sympathetic, like:

PARTNER.   'Oh, I'm sorry babe, that's really annoying.'

HER.   'Annoying'?
I'm fucking livid. 'It's not *annoying*, it's
fundamentally messed up!
It's exactly what we've come to expect from
the Home Office after everything those
dickheads have pulled over the years and it's
calculated and *systemic* and and and *evil!*'
And Man's like:

PARTNER.   (*Does this face.*) '???'

HER.   But I continue.
'Yeah, evil, *fucking* evil. Like the very fabric
of this society.
And now they're holding my passport
hostage?
Like – they're *holding* my passport *hostage*!
I mean, who does that? Who does that? Who
even does that?'
And he gives me this look like:

PARTNER.   'Que pasa? I am confusion.'

HER.

And maybe, I 'on't know, maybe he doesn't
say *those exact words*
coz he's a real human and not, of course,
a meme (or Spanish). But these are minor
details! Coz then he picks up my South
African passport, which they sent back with
the letter, and he asks:

PARTNER.

'Why is your name different?'

HER.

Which is weird, right, that's a *weird* question,
so I give him a *weird* look.

PARTNER.

'Your first name's missing here.'

Beat.

HER.

I look down.
'Oh.'
I look down at the passport.
'Oh right.'
My first name *is* missing on my South African
passport.
My first name has always been missing.
And I'd never questioned why.

Music from 'Think' floats back in briefly:

'Let's go back, let's go back.'

TWO

HER.	I'm at my parents'. It's a weekend and I'm in the dining room with Mama. She's separating out a giant bag of mixed kidney beans. Does this quickly, movements becoming automatic. I watch. I listen. There's a kind of musicality to it. The rattle of all the beans as she scoops them all out of the giant bag. Then the sound of each different coloured bean landing in its designated separate area. White beans in one bowl. Red beans in another. Then the unwanted black beans in a separate disposable bag. White, red, black – scoop. White, red, black – scoop. White – red – black.
HER.	'Mama, quick question: how come my name's missing on all my old passports?'
MAMA.	'Hm!'
HER.	She makes this sound.
MAMA.	'Mm-hm!'
HER.	And I know what's coming.
MAMA.	'Big girl! So you are just sitting there like that, eh? Watching your Mama, like those two hands of yours are just for decoration?'
HER.	(*Mumbles.*) 'Alright Ma, drag me then.' I immediately make myself useful.

Scoop up the beans, start separating them with
her. And then she says:

MAMA.   'Let me tell you about Mobutu.'

HER.   (*Whining*.) 'Nawwwh Mama, not again man.'

She had a tendency, when asked a question,
to go into long tangents that then became
metaphors that then became proverbs about
what the lion said to the grasshopper on the
fourth Sunday, before she actually got to the
point.

MAMA.   'You asked me a question. I am answering
your question. And then?'

HER.   I give her the benefit of the doubt. '…Okay.'
I see her ruffling around the cabinet before she
pulls out a folder. Then she puts on this song:

Something like 'Likambo Ya Ngana' by
Franco & Le TP OK Jazz plays.

MAMA.   'Before Mobutu, a loooooooong time ago…'

HER.   And she suckers me in every time.

MAMA.   'There was Mount Nyiragongo. It is now the
world's most active volcano.
But when Kongo Kingdom belonged to its
people, with all the *richest* natural resources
in all the world, it was silent.
When European men came with their guns
and their religion – '

HER.   'Ah yes, a tale as old as time.'

MAMA.   '...something started to stir in the ground.
                 Bubbling. Moving. Waiting.
                 First the Portuguese came, trading goods.
                 And Kongo Kingdom traded with them – she
                 did not think they would take more than they
                 should.'

HER.   (*Faux shock*.) 'But plot twist – they did!'
                 Then Mama gives me this look (the Congolese
                 Mum equivalent of 'why you being a dick for,
                 bruh?').

MAMA.   'And when they decided that free African
                 labour was more valuable than anything else,
                 in came the other *mundeles*, eh? The British,
                 French, Dutch, under the cloak of night,
                 taking her children – *bana mboka* – sons
                 and daughters of the land – away on ships
                 to build what they called – '

HER.   'The 'new world'!'

MAMA.   (*Sharply*.) 'Who is telling this story?'

HER.   I mind my business. She continues.

MAMA.   'As Kongo tried to move forward, in came
                 another man, a curious thing they called
                 'Stanley something or other'.
                 This Welsh-born American *ndoki*, coming all
                 the way from that new world they forced her
                 children to build. This 'Stanley' saw all her
                 riches and wanted *all of them*.
                 So he went to other men from Europe to
                 decide her fate.
                 They took her name, they took her voice, and
                 they dug and they dug and they tried to take
                 her *power* from the ground.

Making her the private property of a Belgian
King, they decided what he did with her
would be his private business.
And do you know what he did?'

HER.   'Massacred some ten to fifteen million
Congolese,' I say.
And then Mama pauses briefly. A sad smile
spreads across her lips.

MAMA.   '"*Some* ten to fifteen million." African deaths.
Always estimations.
Never recorded fact. Is that not curious?'

Beat.

'But yes. "Some ten to fifteen million"
Congolese deaths.
And as Kongo watched the river that flowed
across her Kingdom turn red with the blood
of her children, something continued to stir in
the ground.
And as the world remained silent, something
continued to bubble, to *move*.
And as they cut down sons and daughters who
fought for her independence, and replaced
them with men who would let them exploit
and pillage and rape and take and take just to
cling to power –
the river of blood flooded the land,
lava erupted from the ground,
and a powerful voice said:
"We are *not* done yet."

Beat.

'So, let me tell you about Mobutu.
Because his story is not in isolation.

When he came into power and said he was
denouncing colonial influences – *le retour à
l'authenticité!* – we rejoiced.
When he changed the country's name to Zaire,
we rejoiced.
When he banned the use of European
Christian names in favour of our traditional
African names, we – all of us – *rejoiced*.

But by the time you were born, after *two*
decades, we knew the truth.
He was another puppet disguised as a hero.
But this ban on names was still in place. So!
(*With mischief.*) What did your Mama and
Papa do, eh? We gave you a Christian name!
(*Smiles.*)
But do not be fooled, *mwana*. It was not
"European influences".
It was our act of rebellion.
When you find your power in the chaos –
however small – no one can take that away
from you. Understand?'

HER.   Then she hands me the folder.

MAMA.   'So your name as you know it – the name
              we gave you and made sure you were to be
              known by – was not allowed to exist. Not on
              your birth certificate. Not on your passport.
              Not on any of your legal documents.'

              Beat.

HER.   'Well *shit*.' I'm shook. I look at Mama and see
              her smiling at me.

MAMA.   'Big girl. It has taken you twenty-six years to
              ask me this question, eh?'

HER.   (*Ruffled, mumbling*.) 'Yeah alright Ma, relax.'

MAMA.   'Keep asking. Understand? *You are not done yet.*'

'Let's go back, let's go back, let's go way, oh, way back when.'

THREE

HER.   Typical. She'd given me an answer that only
              raised more questions.
              But it was also a reminder. Of the Congo I
              was born into.
              A Congo that was inserted into a relationship
              with the West at the very moment of
              decolonisation.
              A Congo that was never allowed to fully come
              into her independence.
              A Congo that grits her teeth when the same
              nations who benefit from keeping her in
              a state of chaos will label her a 'shithole
              country'.

              Beat.

              A Congo that's had more name changes than
              P Diddy (six, yo).

              So my name wasn't allowed to exist,
              in the dream we fought for that turned into
              a nightmare.
              A name that was once a symbol of
              subjugation, became an act of resistance.
              A name that wasn't allowed to exist –
              defied its way into existence.

              Beat.

              The dichotomy of my relationship with
              Congo. My motherland.
              The place of my birth.
              Mine, and yet – not mine.
              We left when I was a baby.
              Everything I know of her, I've learned from
              outside of her.
              There is no personal, living memory.

But in its place is a different kind.
A memory that runs in my blood.

Congo lives on in my 'elsewheres'.

'Elsewheres' that now started to unravel,
started to shift
coming alive like she'd set them aflame.
'Elsewheres' that felt so jarringly different on
the surface.
But then you dig a little deeper. Right?
You dig a little deeper
and start to realise that they were all built by
the same architect.
You dig a little deeper
and you start to see the same soil, same
foundation, same structures holding them up.
Cracked, rusty, rotting away underneath –
but standing.

Beat.

Still standing.

FOUR

HER.   I'm on a train ride home. The folder of
              documents Mama gave me pokes out of my
              bag. I pull it out. Hold it against my chest.
              And think back to that mixed bag of kidney
              beans.
              Think back to that process of separation.
              The rules. The rhythm.
              White, red, black – scoop.
              Rinse. Repeat. 'Til it's automatic.
              Second nature.

              I think back to that curious thing they called
              the 'new world'.
              And what happened in the process of creating
              it.
              What rules were set?
              Which rhythms were followed?
              What became automatic, second nature?
              And why?

              I think back to the conversations I've had with
              friends

THEM.   *'Just for argument's sake.'*

HER.   when I would point out that it was in the
              process of building this 'new world'

THEM.   *'Just hear me out, okay – '*

HER.   that Europeans became White

THEM.   *'Hang on just a second – '*

HER.   and Africans became Black

THEM.   *'It's actually not that simple.'*

HER.   and everyone else became Red, Yellow or
                    Brown.

THEM.   *'You're making it sound simple and it's not.'*

HER.   Because they needed justification.

THEM.   *'Just for argument's sake.'*

HER.   Europe was growing in wealth from the slave
                    trade

THEM.   *'Just for argument's sake.'*

HER.   and they needed justification for the violence

THEM.   *'And I'm just playing devil's advocate.'*

HER.   the theft

THEM.   *'Really, that's all I'm doing here.'*

HER.   the torture

THEM.   *'Playing devil's advocate.'*

HER.   the debasement

THEM.   *'Just don't think it has anything to do with
                    that.'*

HER.   the exploitation

THEM.   *'Why – '*

HER.   the humiliation

THEM.   *'Why – '*

HER.   the complete and utter enslavement of
                   millions of African people.

THEM.   *'Why does it always have to be about race?'*

                   .

HER.   Does anyone have a Bible?
                   The Book of Genesis, King James Version?
                   Specifically, chapter nine, verse eighteen to
                   twenty-seven?

                   She goes into the audience.

                   Hello. Hi. Do you have a Bible with you?

                   *If anyone says 'yes', she plays with this,
                   saying:*
                   *'Okay. So. Here's the thing – sort of planned
                   this whole bit based on you saying 'no', so
                   I'ma need you to try that one again. (Waits.)
                   So, 'no', huh?'*

                   *Roots around in her pockets, taking out a
                   folded page.*

                   Don't worry, I *got* you, okay?
                   Ripped the page out earlier
                   (forgive me Lord, I did it all for theatre).
                   Alright. Here we go!

                   Puts on a booming voice:

                   'And the sons of Noah that went forth from
                   the ark were Shem and Ham and Japheth.

                   And Noah began to be a man of the soil, and
                   he planted a vineyard.

And he drank of the wine, and was drunken;
and he was uncovered within his tent.

And Ham, the father of Canaan, saw the
nakedness of *his* father Noah
and told his two brethren outside.

And Shem and Japheth took a garment and
laid it upon both their shoulders, and went
backward and covered the nakedness of their
father; and their faces were turned away, and
they saw not their father's nakedness.

And Noah awoke from his wine and knew
what his younger son had done unto him.

And he said:
"Cursed be Canaan! A servant of servants
shall he be unto his brethren."'

Beat.

This. This 'sacred text'… is what was used
to justify the enslavement of millions in the
new world.

Beat.

We can unpack the other stuff in a minute, but
firstly can we just talk about how *narratively*
problematic this shit actually is?

So, lemme just recap real quick: your son sees
you butt *neked* – (and one would think that'd
be traumatising enough for anyone's child)
but to get 'vengeance' on him (why were
you butt neked, my dude?) you curse your
grandson instead of the son who saw you butt
neked?

Make it make sense!? Because the maths *ain't
mathing*.

Beat.

Humans are a funny bunch though, aren't we?
We can make anything mean whatever the hell
we want it to mean.
A lie becomes the truth when enough people
believe it to be true.
So in this text, this sacred text, where the
colour of skin is never mentioned, Canaan
was 'interpreted' to have black skin.
So it was then 'believed' that Noah's curse
was a curse against all humans with dark skin.
'Divine will.'
And because nowhere in the text did it say
God *removed* this curse –
slavery was to exist forever.

Beat.

It was in the process of building this new
world that people were set apart by skin
colour.

THEM.   *'It's really not that simple.'*

HER.   Identified in contrast to each other –

THEM.   *'Africans had slaves too, so you can't really
               say it was just Europe's fault.'*

HER.   …and ranked to form a system based on this
               new concept called 'race'.

THEM.   *'And what about the caste system in India?
               That was long before.'*

HER.   A ranking process was now added to *global*
                human existence unlike anything before, and
                we were all cast into it.

THEM.   *'Just don't think...'*

HER.   From the dominant white caste to the lowest
                black caste.

THEM.   *'...that it has anything to do with that.'*

HER.   Assigned roles to meet the needs of a
                production we had no say in.

THEM.   *'Why – '*

HER.   So the stage was set.

THEM.   *'Why – '*

HER.   The house was built.

THEM.   *'Why – '*

HER.   And we would all play our parts.

THEM.   *'Why does it always have to be about race?'*

THREAD TWO
South Africa: Kwerekwere

ONE

'Freedom is Coming' by Khanyo Maphumulo starts playing.
Another 'elsewhere' unravels and comes alive for HER.
She doesn't register the words of the letter.

PASSPORT
OFFICE.   *'Dear Miss Her Last Name*

Our records show that we have not received
a response from you in regards to your
name. Your application to renew your British
passport will not be processed until this is
resolved.

We look forward to hearing from you soon.

Yours sincerely,
Her Majesty's Passport Office.'

HER.   When I get home, I take out the documents
Mama gave me.
I see a name. Mine. Yet not mine.
I see a date. October. 1994.
I see a place. KwaZulu-Natal. South Africa.

The first line of the song's chorus (in Xhosa)
kicks in.

My first elsewhere.

.

When Mobutu started moving mad and there
was talk of civil war,
my parents were like 'nah, peaced out son'
and took me and my two older brothers to live
in South Africa.
Two older brothers who I loved – and
eventually, even grew to quite like
(once your girl could *finesse* TV remote
negotiations, innit).

We didn't have a lot, but had the means of
making a home elsewhere.
We were lucky. Not everyone could say the
same.
Papa was a doctor. Mama started up a small
boutique.
Soon we moved from a small place in Natal
to a nice house in the BaSotho region of
Free State – and into an area they called
'*QwaQwa*'.
Life was sweet. This was our home now.
And we were here to *stay*!

She steps into the 'Freedom is Coming' dance
from Sarafina!
It feels familiar. Easy.
She smiles – feeling herself.
The lyrics in English kick in.

The energy picks up while she dances,
speaking over the music.

It was five months after Mandela became
president.
Six months after Apartheid fully – officially! –
ended.
The country was finally being run by *Black*
South Africans!

Listen! We arrived right after the Happily
Ever After.
Right after Mandela declared 'what is past is
past'.
Right after it became 'the rainbow nation'
where all were 'truly equal'.
And right after a long and brutal fight against
one of the most *sophisticated* forms of
structural racism.

Beat.

Now try and tell me that ain't *beautiful*
timing?

'*Freedom is coming tomorrow...*'

*She stands with one raised fist above her
head, moving it in slow circular motions as we
reach the song's euphoric finale.
Her smile begins to fade.
When the song reaches its conclusion, she
freezes – fist still raised.*

TWO

Film and TV theme tunes soundtracked my
childhood in South Africa.
The first was from *Sarafina!* The story of the
1976 Soweto Uprising when Black school
children took to the streets in protest of
Apartheid.
Police responded with live bullets. At school
children.

I watched this film all the time,
because it had songs and dancing
and I thought it was a fun musical.
I didn't have the words for the feeling I got in
the pit of my stomach,
something hot inside me – bubbling, moving –
at the parts when suddenly it wasn't a fun
musical.
At the scary loud parts.
At the scarier quiet parts.
At the pain of a struggle so violent, you could
feel it in your core.
I was five. Maybe six. And I didn't have the
words.

If you're questioning my parents' decision to
let me watch this so young…
yeah, you're not alone my friend. This, plus
Shaka Zulu and the *sangoma* witch doctor we
called 'White Eyes' fucked me *up*. I was too
scared to go anywhere alone (which made
going to the bathroom a special kind of hell).

But nightmares aside, I'm glad they did.
Sarafina! taught me about Apartheid.
Shaka Zulu taught me about British
imperialism.

We weren't taught this at school.
Almost as if now that the fight was won,
no one wanted to rehash the painful history.
So they skimmed over it.

We were the 'born-frees!' we were told.
Didn't need to worry about what had come
before, we were told.

'What is past is past,' we were told.

THREE

AFRIKANER TEACHER.	'You're different.'

HER.   I'd hear those words a lot. When I lived in all
                       my 'elsewheres'.

AFRIKANER
TEACHER.   'You're different.'

HER.   And I'd look up at my Afrikaner Primary
                       schoolteacher and ask: 'Different how?'

AFRIKANER
TEACHER.   'You're not like the others.'

                       Beat.

HER.   And I'd think... Did she *know*?

                       A foreboding sound begins.

                       Did she know?

                       The sound gets more and more tense.

                       Did she know my secret?

                       *The sound turns into the recognisable theme
                       music from* Dawson's Creek.

                       Did she know of the hours I spent watching
                       Dawson's Creek back to back for Pacey Witter
                       and Pacey Witter only?

                       Theme music from Days of our Lives *plays as
                       she dramatically mimes the words: 'Like sand*

through the hourglass, so are the days of our lives.'

Did she know of my *Days of Our Lives* ritual with Mama every weekday at 5 p.m.?

Theme music from Power Rangers: Time Force *plays*.

Did she know of *Power Rangers: Time Force* every Saturday, coz I was *living* for the messy love triangle between the Pink Ranger, the Red Ranger and her dead ex-fiancé from the future who had *the same face*?

Theme music from Saved by the Bell *plays*.

Did she know that every Sunday I practised at the church of Lisa Turtle?

Theme music from Buffy the Vampire Slayer *plays*.

Did she know about *BUFFY*!? Did she *know* about –

AFRIKANER
TEACHER.   'You're just different. Even the way you speak, it's different.'

HER.   These shows. These *hella white* shows...
had infiltrated my voice
and shaped what became my accent.
I was a Congolese girl, living in South Africa,
who spoke like an American.

.

SOUTH AFRICAN
TEACHER.   '*Mara wena*, you are different.'

HER.   This one hits different.

                  It's a different thing to be seen as 'different'
                  from other Black people by Black people.

SOUTH AFRICAN
TEACHER.   '*Mara wena*, you are not like the others.'

HER.   This came up again. And again and again.
                  And I pushed it aside. I was a kid.
                  I didn't think I had to pay attention to it.
                  None of us did.

                  Beat.

                  We should have.

FOUR

HER.   *Kwerekwere* was a funny word.
            I always thought it was a funny word coz it
            sounded made up, right?
            It means 'foreigner'.
            It sounded like a funny word.

            Beat.

            Until it wasn't.

            .

            We would leave South Africa when I was ten.
            There was so much I didn't have the words to
            say to my South Africans.
            So much I'd be grateful for. In the face of
            impossible odds, Black South Africans fought
            back, danced in defiance and chanted songs of
            freedom until they finally won it.

            And I wanted to hold them. My South African
            brothers and sisters.
            Wanted to hold them and tell them I
            understood. They'd fought so hard. Went
            through so much. I wanted to tell them…
            I wanted to tell them –

THEM.   *'So what happened then?'*

HER.   I wanted to tell them –

THEM.   *'Why did you decide to leave?'*

HER.   I wanted to tell them that I hated this part of
            the story.

THEM.   *'What actually happened?'*

HER.	Papa left for work one night.
THEM.	*'And then what happened?'*
HER.	Two men called out to him.
THEM.	*'What did they say?'*
HER.	That word again. Funny until it wasn't.
THEM.	*'What word?'*
	She says nothing.
	'What word?'
HER.	*'Kwerekwere.'*
THEM.	*'And then what?'*
	She says nothing.
	'And then what?'
HER.	And then they tried to crack open his skull.

Beat.

This is the part of the story I used to leave out.
Because I thought it was the distraction story.
The 'look what Africans will do to each other
if we let them have power' story. The 'Black
on Black crime is just as much to blame' story.
It's only in telling it that I remember why we
should never leave out parts of our history.
No matter how ugly or painful.
It's only in telling it that I see the patterns in
the chaos.
They're always there.

I guess the thing about inheriting an old house
is that you inherit *all* of it.
The soil, the foundation, the structures
holding it up.
And you can move in straight away, feng shui
the place
make it look nice at first glance and show it
off to your friends.
But if you don't get someone in to examine
the damage
and acknowledge the problems they find at the
root
then do the hard, taxing, unglamorous work
of fixing it before you move in
you haven't really changed as much as you
think you've changed.
You're still just living in an old house.

It was said: 'What is past is past.'
Yet the past was still the present.
Poor Black South Africans living in
destitution before Apartheid were still living
in destitution when Apartheid was over.
White Afrikaners still held the economic
power.
The racist police state was still racist
even if the majority of officers were now
Black.
All of this was known, yet no one wanted to
acknowledge it.

Maybe because acknowledging it would be
admitting that the freedom they fought so hard
to win wasn't what they thought it would be.

This was what we arrived into when we
moved to 'QwaQwa'.
One of the smallest and poorest former
homelands.

We arrived into the world of Black South
Africans who were unseen and forgotten
in a country they had finally won back from
white rule,
only to watch other Africans emigrate over
and start to gain all the things they still
couldn't –
because of the very history of their country.

We thought we'd escaped Apartheid.
But Apartheid still haunted South Africa.
Like a ghost in an old house.
You couldn't progress without exorcising the
ghost or moving away.

Beat.

So we moved away.
And I was *gutted*, man.

Beat.

I'd only just started *Gilmore Girls*.

Theme music from Gilmore Girls *plays into
the next scene.*

THREAD THREE
Ireland: Black Girl

ONE

PASSPORT
OFFICE.   *'Dear Miss Her Last Name*

*We have still not received a response from
you. Please note that your application will be
terminated if we do not hear from you soon.*

*Yours sincerely,
Her Majesty's Passport Office.'*

HER.   A Congolese girl moves to Ireland via South
Africa just one month after she gains South
African citizenship.
She wonders about the irony of having proof
of your legitimacy in a country where no one
cares.
Do the Irish have a word for *kwerekwere* here?

She soon realises they don't need one.
When everywhere you go, everything you see,
everyone you meet
is a reminder of what you are not.

You are not a redhead.
But your hair juts out with a boldness they
will never know.
You do not have flowing tresses.
But your curls coil up with a tightness they
will never know.
You do not have green/blue eyes.

But your brown ones hold a depth they will
never know.
You do not have delicate lips.
But your wide lips stand out with a fullness
they will never know.
You do not have fair skin.
But your skin, but your skin, *your skin*.

Beat.

When they tell you they were slaves too
that they know your pain,
that they share your history
you smile a tight-lipped smile and hold your
tongue,
the tongue that wants to remind them that
indentured servants with basic rights
and African slaves with none,
were not one and the same.
But you're ten. Maybe eleven.
And you don't have the words yet
but something inside you is *stirring,* twisting.

When they reach for your hair without pause,
you let them
waiting for that moment of horror, of surprise,
of disgust
when their light hands make contact with your
thick creams and your heavy oils, and your
full-bodied moisturisers.

Then you wait for the blame to come.
And it always does.

In a little town called Ennis, in County Clare,
Ireland
there you are.

Black Girl. I see you.

With your hair that juts out with a boldness
they will never know.
With your curls that coil up with a tightness
they will never know.
With your brown eyes that hold a depth they
will never know.
With your wide lips that stand out with a
fullness they will never know.
With your skin, with your skin, *with your skin*.

Black Girl. You are beautiful.
God, how I wish you knew.

TWO

HER.   By the time we moved to Ireland, I'd gained
              a little brother. My little friend.
              He arrived six years ago, taking my place at
              the bottom of the hierarchy. We love to see it.
              But he was adorable. And lovely.
              And smelled of kindness, if kindness had
              a smell.
              Once on our way home from primary school,
              he went missing.
              I thought he'd just nipped round to a friend's
              without telling me.
              When I got home and told Mama, I'll never
              forget the look on her face.

              There was fear, yeah. But there was also
              something else.
              Something more.
              Like something dragged up from somewhere
              else was coming out of her.
              Like she'd lived this before and was dreading
              when it would come again.
              That's when I realised what our mothers carry
              with them.
              Every second of every day. The dread. The
              inevitability.
              The grief that isn't theirs but they've felt it
              like their own so many times until it became
              their own.

              He turned up later that day. My little brother.
              All smiles.
              Said he'd nipped round to a friend's house and
              forgot to tell me.

              The little *shit*.

THREAD FOUR
Wigan: Anthony

ONE

PASSPORT
OFFICE.   *'Dear Miss Her Last Name,*
                Why the fuck won't you answer us?'

HER.   …Sorry?

PASSPORT
OFFICE.   *'Are you having a fucking laugh?'*

HER.   Come again?

PASSPORT
OFFICE.   *'We will FUCK you UP if you don't comply.*

                Yours sincerely,
                Her Majesty's Passport Office.'

HER.   *Wow.*

                Beat.

                So… maybe, I 'on't know, that wasn't actually
                what the letter said,
                but that's what it *felt* like, right, that's what it
                felt like when I read it.
                So I call 'em up! Ready to give 'em hell, put
                on my 'Nice White Lady on the Phone' voice
                and tell them to back the fuck up because I
                was *working through something* after the path
                they'd sent me down and I needed time, okay,
                I needed *time*. And so I speak to someone, I

speak to someone and it's this scouse bloke
and he's called Steven and he's... delightful?
Fucking *delightful*! (I know, very anti-
climatic).

Turns out, Steven's been assigned to my case
and his boss is breathing down his neck and
all Steven needs me to do is send him an
email, not even a letter, *just* an email saying
I received the letter and I am in the middle
of sorting out my name. So I do it, there and
then, and at this point, we're hella tight, me
and Steven, so I'm like:

'Ste. *My dude!* Let me tell you about
Mobutu...'

TWO

> *'Confessions Part II' by Usher plays as she starts grooving.*

HER.   So! Papa gets a new job and we move to Wigan… around about the time Usher read himself for filth and came out with an album of reasons why Chilli should *throw the whole man* away.

And why did *this* album soundtrack a Congolese family moving from a small town in Ireland to North-West England?
Come on, man!

> *Beat.*

It slaps, innit.

> *Lip-syncing the lyrics:* **'And I don't know what to do, I guess I gotta give you part two of my confessions'** *then music stops abruptly.*

Wigan was funny, man. It started off innocently enough.

THEM.   *'Why is your English so good?'*

HER.   So, do I tell them about *Dawson's Creek*, or…?

THEM.   *'How come you're so smart?'*

HER.   I think that's a compliment… right?

THEM.   *'Your nails are actually really clean.'*

HER.   Now I'm really struggling, my dude.

THEM.   *'Is that actually your... own... work?'*

HER.   Can you tell your Year Eight teacher to fuck-
             off, or nah?

THEM.   *'You didn't... copy it... from anywhere, did
             you?'*

HER.   What is this?

THEM.   *'Because if you did, you can tell the truth.'*

HER.   Seriously, what is this?

THEM.   *'You're different.'*

             Beat.

HER.   No.

THEM.   *'You're different.'*

HER.   Nah, not this.

THEM.   *'You're different.'*

HER.   Not this again.

THEM.   *'You're not like the others.'*

HER.   *Who* are 'the others'?
             The other Blacks? The other troublemakers?
             The other criminals?
             The other idiots and losers and thugs and
             lazies and beasts and savages and rapists
             and every other bullshit dangerous lie that
             has been repeated about Black people for
             centuries until it seeped into the very air

we breathe and embedded itself into our
subconscious like it was fact?

When enough people believe a lie, it can seem
like the truth.
And anything that goes against this lie is
deemed 'different.'
I want to say it. Go to say it. It's there. It's in
me. Bursting to get out.

PUPIL 1.   *'Was really sad, that, weren't it?'*

HER.   And then it happens.

PUPIL 2.   *'Yeah, shockin', really.'*

HER.   I hear about it.

PUPIL 1.   *'So sad.'*

HER.   I hear about you.

PUPIL 2.   *'So close by too.'*

HER.   And I see your picture.

PUPIL 1.   *'That's what's scary, innit?'*

HER.   And you look like my little brother.
                Same smile.
                Same dark skin.

PUPIL 2.   *'Was there the other day me, y'know?'*

HER.   And somewhere inside me, I know that you
                actually were. My brother.

PUPIL 1.   *'Some right wrong 'uns out there.'*

HER.   With your black blazer.

PUPIL 2.   *'What would make someone do that?'*

HER.   And your sparkling eyes.

PUPIL 2.   *'What would make someone do that though?'*

HER.   And cheeks I bet were squeezed all the time
                by intrusive aunties.

PUPIL 1.   *'Some people are just sick in the head, innit.'*

HER.   I bet you were adorable when you were little.

PUPIL 2.   *'Yeah. Just sick in the head.'*

HER.   I bet you were adorable and lovely
                and smelled of kindness
                if kindness had a smell.

                Beat.

                Anthony.

                Beat.

                I hear about you.
                In a town not so far from Wigan.
                I hear about you.
                And how they cut you down
                and left nothing of you.
                And how they ripped you apart
                because you dared to exist.
                And how they took your light
                like it was theirs to take.
                And I think about your sisters.
                And I think about your brother.
                And I think about your father.

And I think about your *mother*.
And then something, some *thing* in me cracks
open, and I can't –
breathe.
I can't breathe and I don't get why. And
there's something, for a moment, there's
something in me, from before, tightening
inside me, twisting up in my gut, crushing my
insides, I *feel* it.

Then I hear screaming. Someone's screaming
like it's coming from their soul. Like it's being
dragged up from somewhere else and ripped
out of them and it hurts and I don't know how,
but I know that it *hurts*, and then I realise it's
me.

I'm the one screaming.

THREAD FIVE

London Part 1: Love

ONE

HER.   A Congolese girl moves to London
                via Wigan via Ireland via South Africa
                and is 'naturalised' a British citizen for the
                first time.
                She wonders what it means to be 'naturalised'
                in this country
                awash in blood
                that now carried her worth in a tiny red
                booklet?
                She wonders if this red booklet
                'requests and requires in the name of Her
                Majesty'
                that airport security leave her the fuck alone
                now?
                She wonders how soon her accent,
                with its hints of 'elsewhere',
                will be colonised by this city?
                She wonders who she will become.
                Who she will love.
                And who will choose to love her?

TWO

HER.   When I moved to London, I thought a lot
                about love. Which made sense.
                For someone raised on an unhealthy (and
                frankly, alarming) amount of American
                soap operas and American teen dramas and
                American rom-coms where the line between
                'is this actually any good?' and 'shoot me in
                the fucking face' was *hella* blurry, it made
                sense.

                But I was surprisingly realistic about it.

                You wouldn't find *me* going around *expecting*
                to meet someone by chance at a 'function' and
                have them fall madly in love with me from
                one conversation because – reasons? You
                know?

                I didn't *expect* a gorgeous beautiful man to
                look into my eyes and *just know* how much of
                a fucking catch I am (and listen, I *am*!) based
                on zero discernable evidence beyond *plot*,
                okay?

                I wasn't waiting for a 'meet-cute' where
                sparks would fly and one person just knows
                that this is *'it'*. Right? And maybe a few
                years later this one person who 'just knows'
                happens to meet you again, and it happens to
                just work out, because this one person, they
                happened to be right all along, and slowly
                but surely you let yourself fall – no, not fall,
                *plung*e – fucking plunge into the mammoth
                gigantic overwhelming abyss that is love and
                know that you've found *your person*.

                I didn't go around expecting *that*.

That would be – (*Laughs.*) That would be –
(*Whistles, doing the 'crazy' motion.*)
that would be…

Beat.

…exactly what happened. That. Literally
that. That's how I fell in love, which is almost
annoying –

THEM.   *'So what's it like…'*

HER.   that all these years, *decades* I'd spent
watching these shitty rom-coms and revelling,
right, just *revelling* in how fundamentally
bullshit they all were –

THEM.   *'What's it like…'*

HER.   and my real-life experience of romantic love
plays out exactly like one –

THEM.   (*Suggestively.*) *'What's it like to be with a
Black girl?'*

Beat.

HER.   Right.

THEM.   (*More suggestively.*) *'What's it like to be with
a Black girl?'*

HER.   That's a moodkill, innit?

THEM.   (*Hella suggestively.*) *'What's it like to be with
a Black girl?'*

HER.   I see how *this* never made it into the rom-
coms I watched.

THEM.   (*Obscenely suggestive.*) '*What's it like to be with a Black girl?*'

HER.   Something in me from before stirs up again.
              Twisting, tighter and tighter and knotting up.
              And maybe this time I look to my partner. My
              real-life rom-com person.
              And maybe he looks back at me, in confusion.
              Shifts uncomfortably, realising what's being
              asked of him.
              Maybe he takes his time.
              Maybe this is what he eventually says.

THEM.   '*What's it like to be with a Black girl?*'

PARTNER.   'I don't know. It's wonderful? Joyous. And
              scary, I guess.
              To give so much of yourself to someone and
              have them do the same.
              But that's not the question you're asking, is it?

              It's… getting used to her silk scarf staining
              your pillows with tea tree and castor oil.
              (*Smiles.*) But that's not the question you're
              asking. Is it?

              Beat.

              It's hard. Yeah. It's really hard.
              And maybe it would be easier, if she wasn't
              there.
              Maybe it would be easier to hear one of your
              white friends casually say 'what up, my
              negroes' if she wasn't there with you.
              Maybe it would be easier to not tense up in
              that moment, or hear another friend say 'I'm
              sure he didn't mean it that way.'

Maybe it would be easier to brush it aside,
as just one insignificant, careless moment of
stupidity.
Maybe it would be easier to not go any
further, to not go any deeper,
to not try to understand how a single careless
moment can encapsulate a subtle violence that
is felt by Black people at the hands of white
people.
That second violence after the first – maybe
even worse than the first.
The violence of refusing to acknowledge that
anything significant has happened.

Beat.

Maybe it would be easier if she wasn't there
because I have never had to think about race
so much before in my whole life. Maybe
it would be easier because, selfishly, I'm
scared. Because the more I understand of
what it means to navigate the world as a
Black person, the more I question: if all I can
promise is to *be present* but can never *relate*,
could loving her ever be enough?'

THEM.   *'What's it like to be with a Black girl?'*

She stops.
We see her shift back into herself, taking over.
It is no longer about one single relationship.

HER.   It's shaking yourself out of that fear and
realising you should've been asking 'why
wouldn't I be the one to share the weight
with her?' It's a weight that has rested on the
shoulders of Black people for far too long.

It's knowing the very words you speak are
specific to her and not every Black Girl,
because no one Black Girl can be every
Black Girl.

It's showing up. Every day. Every action,
every word, every time you say something
isn't right you stop the unacceptable from
becoming normal.
You decide who you want to be. Who you
continue to be every day.

So yeah, it's *wonderful*. Joyous. Scary.
And hard.
But how could it not be?
We're chipping away at the foundations of an
old house built long before any of us got here.
We're fighting the poison of an idea given
so much power it ingrained itself into every
system in existence.
So it's *hard*.

Beat.

How could it not be?

THREE

She now takes in the space. Observes the pillars. The giant box.
The volcanic rocks at her feet. Walks around them. Takes her
time.

HER.   It's in this mess –
              in the hard, the scary, the joyous and
              wonderful –
              that I am formed.
              And it's here – in a love that exists within
              this mess –
              that something else begins to
              form in *me*.
              A voice. Both new and familiar, wraps itself
              around me. Holds me.
              The girl without an anchor.
              Roots me to *this place*.
              And demands to be heard.

              She looks around at the volcanic rocks that
              surround her.
              One of the rocks starts to glow. She picks it
              up. Weighs it in her hand.
              Then she walks up to the giant box, her stride
              powerful.
              She uses the rock to carve out her name on the
              box. Then steps back.

              I get my full name printed on my South
              African passport.

THREAD SIX
London Part 2: Another You

ONE

PASSPORT
OFFICE.   *'Dear Miss B. N. Lombe,*

Your application has been successfully
processed and we are delighted to attach
your renewed British passport in the
enclosed envelope. Please sign your passport
immediately.

Yours sincerely,
Her Majesty's Passport Office.'

HER.   So it arrives. Yet by now it had become about
so much more than this.
What's that old cliché – it's the journey, not
the destination?
Still, here it was. Renewed proof of my
legitimacy. My right to exist.
Finally carrying my name, as I'd always
known it.

I hold the envelope in my hands.
Feel the weight.
Think about how truly poetic it is, that the
British passport should be the same deep red
as the colour of blood.
I reach into the envelope, slowly pull it out.
Look down.

Beat.

It's blue now. (Fuck's sake. You couldn't just let me be great?)

TWO

HER.   London was always a race.
I don't remember against who.
Just that I needed to *keep moving*.
As fast as I could.
And key milestones sped by:
The birth of my first nephew. My confidante.
My best friend.
I watch him grow into a spunky, intelligent
ten-year-old kid.
Keep moving.
The birth of my second nephew.
I watch my two older brothers beautifully
juggling fatherhood.
Keep moving.
Get a job. Build a career. Make friends.
Keep moving.
Watch my little bro, who wasn't so little any
more, grow into a man.
Keep moving.
Did his shoulders droop lower?
Keep moving.
Did his smile come slower?
Keep moving.
Had his bright eyes dimmed?
Keep it moving, so you don't feel it growing
inside –
And then I hear about you.
Another you. A different you.
And I feel it again. *There*. Something inside.
Getting worse.

DOCTOR.   'Just take two paracetamol three times a day
and the pain should go away, alright?'

HER.   'Okay? But I think… I think that something
might be *wrong*, maybe?'

DOCTOR.   'It's always much worse in your head, than in reality.'

HER.   'In my head? No, I don't think it's just in my – '

DOCTOR.   'Is that all?'

HER.   'Look, Doctor, I don't wanna sound like I'm – '

DOCTOR.   'Sorry, I have other patients waiting. You understand don't you?'

                .

HER.   It gets worse. Something in there gets *worse*. So I go back.
            'Can you just do some tests? *Any* tests? Please.'

DOCTOR.   'I felt around, and there's nothing that indicates any cause for – '

HER.   'Please.'

DOCTOR.   'We don't even know what we'd be testing for.'

HER.   'I know my body.'

DOCTOR.   'Give it a few weeks, then come in again.'

HER.   'I *know* my body.'

DOCTOR.   'A few weeks. And it'll go away on its own. Just wait and see.'

HER.   I try to distract myself. See friends. Go out. Drink.

Keep moving.

Check in on the family WhatsApp group.

Keep moving.

Open a video of my nephew singing a song about shapes.

Tell my bro he's now *that guy* sending videos of his kids doing dumb shit.

Keep moving.

Watch the video of my nephew singing a song about shapes.

It's… delightful. Watch it over and over and over again.

Keep moving.

Visit my parents. My Mama and Papa.

Who turned a symbol of subjugation into resistance.

What did you have to hold down inside you?

What do you hold down still?

Keep moving.

Wait and see.

Keep moving.

Wait and see.

Keep moving.

Wait!

Keep it *moving* so you don't feel it –

But I do. It's still *there*, knotting and *tangling* and *pulling* inside me, getting heavier and heavier.

And *still* – I'm told to wait. So I wait.

And when I wait, I hear about you.

Another you. A different you.

A you who rode in a minicab. And wore a hoodie. And went to a corner shop. And walked home with Skittles. And played with a toy gun. And waited for a bus. And went for a jog. A you who got a traffic ticket. And went to church. And pulled out a wallet.

A you who ran. A you who didn't.

THEM.   *'Why – '*

HER.   A you who said he couldn't breathe.

THEM.   *'Why – '*

HER.   A you who wanted to live.

THEM.   *'Why – '*

HER.   A you who wanted to live.

THEM.   *'Why does it always have to be about race?'*

HER.   A you who always just wanted to live.

             Beat.

             And then it happens. And time speeds up.
             And it's *here*.
             Something dragged up from somewhere
             else, from all my elsewheres – is coming
             alive inside me. It's *here*. The bubbling and
             moving I have felt all my life is now twisting
             and tangling and *burning* with a tightness.
             It's *here*. A tightness in my gut. Weaving
             and threading and pulling and twisting and
             pushing the air out of me until it feels like
             my insides are spilling out, until it feels like
             my insides are *erupting* out of me like lava.
             Time's up. It's *here*.

             Beat.

             I have emergency surgery.
             I'm told my intestines twisted around
             themselves so tightly
             they were about to burst at any moment.

Beat.

They ask me how I got here.
They ask me how *we* got here.
They ask me how all of it got to *this* stage.

THREE

A news broadcast is heard over real projected footage of
protests as the actor goes back to sit within the audience.

REPORTER.   *'Protests that started in the US city of*
Minneapolis, Minnesota, after the police
killing of an unarmed Black man have erupted
across the globe. During a global pandemic,
we are witnessing one of the largest global
movements against anti-Black racism in
history.

Bristol made international headlines after
protesters pulled down the statue of slave
owner Edward Colston – inspired by the
"Rhodes Must Fall" movement that started
with students in South Africa tearing down the
statue of British imperialist Cecil Rhodes.

In Wales, the town of Denbigh is fiercely
debating whether to remove the statue of
Welsh-born American Henry Morton Stanley,
who famously orchestrated the brutal reign of
King Leopold II over the Congo.

In Belgium, statues of King Leopold II
continue to come down, as the nation "wakes
up" to Belgium's bloody colonial past.

We will continue to report on this story as it
develops.'

EPILOGUE

For My People

Projected title reads: 'Bush Theatre: The Protest.' The name 'Benedict Lombe' appears before the video clip starts to play.

VIDEO.   *'So. As I tried to write these words*
I couldn't help but wonder
about all those times in history when we've
tried to write these words.
About all those times in history when we've
had to take our pain
and our rage and our trauma
and turn it into something articulate and
insightful and poetic.

I repeat:
take our pain and our rage and our trauma
and turn it into something else.

Because this pain and this rage and this
trauma is not articulate or insightful or
poetic.
It's exhausting. It's overwhelming. It's
unrelenting and – and cruel. And unequal.
And all-encompassing. And too much.
And too much. And too much.
And yet here we are. Here I am. Still.
Trying to turn it into something else
like we have done throughout history,
each time,
like we have done throughout history,
each time,
thinking maybe, this time, thinking maybe,
this time, this time, they might finally hear us.'

Video pauses as reviews are stamped over it, accompanied by voices:

JOURNO 1.   'Times *review – "More lecture than theatre." Three stars.'*

JOURNO 2.   'Guardian *review – "A superb set of dramas for the Black Lives Matter movement." Four stars.'*

PRODUCER.   *'Darling! Had to get in touch. Big fan of your work. I just want to be doing something, you know? For the cause.'*

L.A.
PRODUCER.   *'Listen, ever thought about the big screen? That raw pain in your eyes just screams "epic", you know?'*

                   The actor now gets up to stand in front of the empty stage.
                   Music from 'Think' drifts back in - its once upbeat notes now short, sharp and haunting.

HER.   I really struggled with this. Right now, with all of you. I knew it would come.

                   When what was real would turn into artifice.

                   When I would dip into the pain.
                   Resist the very act. Fail.
                   Question who I'm doing it for at every turn.

                   Add more! Add less! Don't be too *intense*!

                   Add songs! And *dancing*! Be fun, Bene.
                   Be relatable, Bene. Be *funnier*!

                   Beat.

No matter how you look at it, or what form it
takes, the fact is this:
Every time we stand up here, we are begging
the world to see our humanity.
Begging the world to stop killing us.

Beat.

'More lecture than theatre.'
I think about that a lot.
About that reaction to something that was by
us and for us.
Something that was dragged up from within
us and given room to be said and heard.
Something that was never intended to be
reviewed as theatrical consumption. I think
about that space we created for ourselves to
gather, to scream, to *hold* each other and how
that notion was still alien. For Black people to
create something about Black pain that wasn't
for non-Black people to be entertained by?

It couldn't not be theatre when we've always
been the protagonists in the theatre of our
tragedy. It couldn't not be theatre with the
long history of our bodies being put on
display. With the daily images of slain Black
bodies.

So where, exactly, is the space we're allowed
to exist in? When either our pain becomes
another piece of content, or we're 'lecturing'.
Preaching too loud. Too strong. With too
much *anger*.

So where do we go? Where do we go with
it? With this anger that has been weaponised
against us for too long, with this rage, with

this fire in our bellies, in our guts, this *searing* hot flame that cannot be put out – where do we go with it? Where is it allowed to exist without judgement? Where is it allowed to be felt and heard and acted upon? Where is it allowed to go to change the very fabric of our world? To light it up 'til it catches fire, to light it up 'til it turns to dust, to light it up 'til it falls away, leaving space for us to create something new from everything we bear witness to? Where is it allowed to go to be expelled from our *souls* so our bodies can be lighter, so our bodies can be so light that our minds can wander as if we live in a world where all our stories are not tied up in our pain?

It is time. It has always been time.

Because what you *see* of where we are right now started long before. What you *feel* of where we are right now started so long before. In the ground. Boiling. Bubbling. Moving. It started as a whisper that turned into a scream that shook up the earth beneath our feet until the pressure forced it to emerge, to erupt, to spill out like hot lava. Lava that cannot be stopped. Because it is time. It has always been time.

Do you feel it? Do you hear it?

Beat.

Do you hear us now?

Lights start to go down. She interrupts this. She is not done yet.

This is usually where I'm supposed to end it.
Right?
With a question for you. A provocation for
you. A challenge for you.
And then what? Will we come back and just
do this again?
Will we come back and just do this all over
again?

Nah. That's not good enough any more.
And to be honest, it never was.

Her voice starts to grow in power.

So this ending is for me. For us.
For my people.
For when our spirits wane. For when our
voices falter. For when words fail us and hope
feels out of reach and grief consumes us and
we forget that our very *existence* is a radical
act and we made the impossible possible and
we learnt to love ourselves and each other
when the world told us we couldn't and we
held each other and we continue to hold each
other and we made love and we made love
and we made LOVE and joy and fucking
magic in the darkness. In the darkness – we
made our own light.

*Projection transforms into a montage of Black
people in moments of love, light, laughter and
joy.*

Black people. My people. We who were
named such to forever keep us in subjugation.
Silent and separate. We who took the names
they gave us and *resisted* everything they
told us about ourselves. We who have come

to know that we are the very language of
difference and magic.

Black people. My people. We who have been
screaming from the very tops of our lungs
that it is not enough to just exist if we can't
exist freely and fully and equally. We who
have kept screaming no matter how many of
us they cut down and tried to silence. We who
have used our rage and our pain and our grief
as fuel to burn down the walls of a house that
was never built for us to thrive in. We who
said *we are not done yet.*

Black people! My people. We who have
redefined culture with our talent and our wit
and our *sauce*. We who not only dared to
imagine a new house but dared to start laying
the foundations. We who invite you now to
join us in building this new house but warn
you that we will not wait. We will not wait for
anyone. We who refuse to wait – ever again.
Because it is time. It has always been time.

Children of the land! *Bana mboka! (Laughs.)*
Yes, my Congolese people.
Yes, my African people.
Yes, my *Black* people.

I see you. I *thank* you.
In your resistance, you have kept me alive.
In your resistance, you have given me a voice.
In your resistance, I have found my *true*
name.

The road is still long, but we've come so far.
This road has been long. But you lot, yeah?
(She looks around with pride.)

Beat.

You lot, man!

A phone video of her young nephew is projected on-screen.
He is singing a song about shapes. Badly.
She turns to watch him with us.
He momentarily gets distracted by the front-facing camera and starts to play with his face.
She laughs.
He goes back to the song with more gusto.
She watches him until the very end.

It is pure, unadulterated Black joy.

And this is where we choose to end it.

End.

A Nick Hern Book

Lava first published in Great Britain as a paperback original in 2021 by Nick Hern Books Limited, The Glasshouse, 49a Goldhawk Road, London W12 8QP, in association with the Bush Theatre, London

Cover photograph by Latoya Fits Okuneye, Art Direction by Doug Kerr, Wardrobe provided by Tina Lobondi.

Designed and typeset by Nick Hern Books, London
Printed in Great Britain by Mimeo Ltd, Huntingdon, Cambridgeshire PE29 6XX

A CIP catalogue record for this book is available from the British Library

ISBN 978 1 83904 009 2

www.nickhernbooks.co.uk

facebook.com/nickhernbooks

twitter.com/nickhernbooks